What's My Family Tree?

Mick Manning
and Brita Granström

W

FRANKLIN WATTS
LONDON·SYDNEY

For Max with love from Mum and Dad

This edition 2005

Franklin Watts, 338 Euston Road
London, NW1 3BH

Franklin Watts Australia
Level 17/207 Kent Street
Sydney, NSW 2000

Text and illustrations © 2001
Mick Manning and Brita Granström

The illustrations in this book were made by Mick and Brita
Find out more about Mick and Brita on www.mickandbrita.com

Editor: Rachel Cooke
Art director: Jonathan Hair

Printed in China
A CIP catalogue record is available
from the British Library.

Dewey Classification 306.8
ISBN 978 0 7496 5664 5

Franklin Watts is a division of Hachette Children's Books,
an Hachette Livre UK company.
www.hachettelivre.co.uk

Contents

4

What's my family tree?

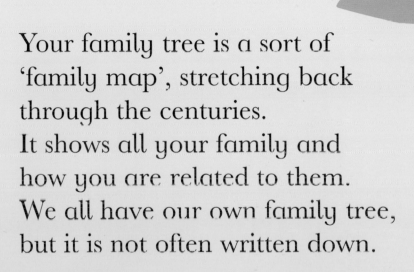

Your family tree is a sort of 'family map', stretching back through the centuries.
It shows all your family and how you are related to them.
We all have our own family tree, but it is not often written down.

Why is it called a family tree?

Because families join together when people have children or get married, so the map grows a new part or branch – it starts to look a bit like a tree . . .

And where do I fit in?

You're a new name on the family map – a sort of new shoot on your family tree. You are joined to a branch that's your mum and dad!

Mum

Ask Mum or Dad to show you pictures of when they were young.

Dad

What about Mum and Dad?

Your mum and dad were babies once, too! They both came from different families, each with its own family tree.

8

One day they met each other and became friends. Perhaps they lived together, or got married. Then, after a while, they had a baby and that was the beginning of your family branch!

Do we all have a mum and dad?

Yes, we all need to have a dad when we are made – and we need a mum to grow inside! They are Mum and Dad – our birth parents.

Sometimes, children don't stay with their birth parents but are adopted. Their adopted parents become Mum and Dad instead.

Why did Mum and Dad want a baby?

Well that's difficult to answer! But most people have a baby because they love each other very much and know that their baby will be a mixture of them both.

Why do I look like I do?

You are unique – there has never been anyone like you before in the world! But you inherit qualities from your parents, from the way you look to the way you think.

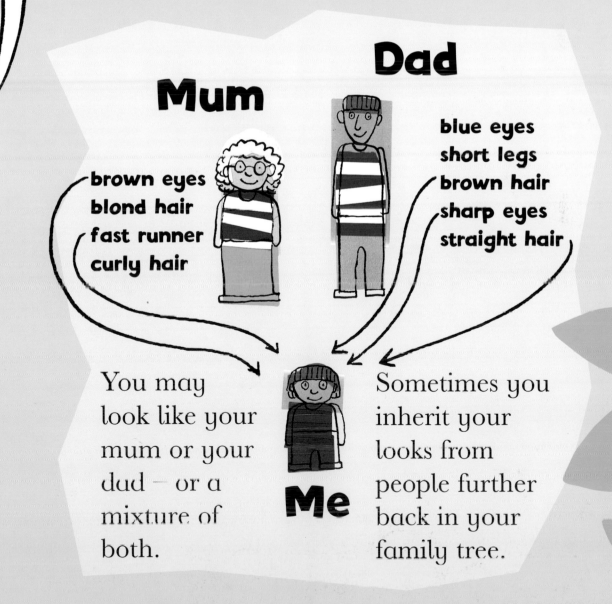

Mum

brown eyes
blond hair
fast runner
curly hair

Dad

blue eyes
short legs
brown hair
sharp eyes
straight hair

Me

You may look like your mum or your dad – or a mixture of both.

Sometimes you inherit your looks from people further back in your family tree.

Why am I good at things Mum and Dad can't do?

Well, maybe it's just natural talent – part of being uniquely you! Or maybe you get it from one 'side' of the family? Just like your looks, you can inherit talents from grandparents or ancestors from long ago!

Great-great-great-great-grandpa Ravi

Great-great-aunty Vita

So when you suddenly show a talent for football or painting, sometimes your family can't think where it comes from!

Great-grandpa Stanley

Great-great-granny Dora

Do you take after someone in particular?

Great-great-auntie Ingrid

Great-great-great-uncle Albert

So what's a family then?

A family usually means Mum and Dad and their children – you and any brothers and sisters (your siblings) you may have. They are your 'close' family.

Brothers and sisters are children who have the same parents as you. Half-brothers or half-sisters are siblings that share one parent with you – that's when Mum or Dad has had a baby with someone else.

There is no such thing as a 'normal' family. A family can be all sorts of different mixtures: Dad and his friend; Mum and her partner; Auntie Sue and Cousin Jack; maybe your gran or grandad look after you a lot.

It doesn't matter what your close family is like, just so long as you all love and look after each other.

17

What are one-parent families?

Sometimes mums and dads split up. They don't want to live together any more and one of them moves out. Children often then get two homes – one to live in and one to visit in the holidays.

Sadly, too, sometimes either Mum or Dad dies. The other parent is left on their own with the children.

And why don't some children live with their real parents?

Sometimes parents can't look after their children, even though they may want to. Then the children can be looked after by foster parents for a while. But sometimes these children are adopted by other parents forever – and become a new shoot on a different family tree.

What about other relatives – cousins and things?

Your relatives are all the people on your family tree. If your mum and dad have any brothers or sisters, they are your uncles and aunts. If your uncles and aunts have any children, they are your cousins!

Aunt (Dad's brother's wife) Uncle (Dad's brother) Dad Mum Aunt (Mum's sister) Uncle (Mum's sister's husband)

Cousin Cousin Cousin Me Cousin Cousin

Relatives like this are some of the nearest
of the other branches on your family tree.
They may live nearby – or in a far-away country!

So what are my grans and grandads?

Grans and grandads are our mum's mum and dad, and our dad's mum and dad. You have four of them on your family tree.

Why have I only one grandad?

Some grans and grandads may be dead – but they are remembered on your family tree.

Ask to see some photos of them . . .

So who were my great-grandparents?

Your great-grandparents were your gran's and grandad's mums and dads, so you've got eight of them! They were born a long time ago.

It's like a history story!

Try saying 'great-grandad' then add some more greats at the beginning . . .
Each great goes back about 25 years – the more greats you add, the further back in history you go!

Granny & Grandad

Great-great-great-great-granny & grandad

Great-great-great-great-great-great-granny & grandad

great-
great-
great-
great-
great-great-
great-great-
great...

Great x 16 granny & grandad

Great x 26 granny & grandad

Great x 46 granny & grandad

Great x 500 granny & grandad

You can usually trace your family tree back about 200 years. After that, just imagine who your relatives might have been!

25

Will my family tree keep growing?

Yes! It's growing all the time. Your mum and dad may have more children. And perhaps when you grow up, you will have a baby. But right now you're the fresh, new shoot, on the brand new branch, on your very, very old family tree . . .

And remember this . . .

A family tree

Great-grandparents

Great-grandparents

Great-aunt Great-uncle

Gran and Grandad

Great-uncle
and lots of children I can't fit in!

Uncle Aunt

Uncle's
ex

Uncle

Aunt

Aunt's
ex

Mum

Cousin Cousin

Cousin Cousin

These
cousins are
stepbrothers
and
stepsister

Stepcousin

Brother

A family tree looks like this. Why not draw your own
and see how many branches you can fill in?